Buying an original Copyright indie publication ensures creative content, endorses forward thinking and vision, encourages public action, and recognizes and furthers the human condition. Thank you for buying my book and recognizing Copyright infringement by not reproducing, scanning or distributing without permission. Your support is valued and necessary.

U.S. Copyright ©
Me and Jo and a Black Cat named Tupelo
January 6th, 2022
Spartaghina LLC

FORWORD

As I state in the book, I grew up with dogs
and cats, and presently share my house with
two kooky toms, each with its own distinct
personality. My mother always said that I have
a soft heart; we share the same adoration for
animals, even after a dog severely bit me when I
was twelve years old. It wasn't the dog's fault.
He was simply a young overly excited puppy.
I know it was an accident.

I believe dogs and cats were put on earth to help
humans cope, entertain us, and provide comfort.
In return, these treasured animals require a few
modest things: love and attention, food, shelter,
and a trip to the vet occasionally. The trade-off is
well worth the minor challenges of owning a pet.
(Nobody is perfect)

I hope you enjoy the message and cherish your
pets throughout their short lives.

What are Half rhymes or Imperfect rhymes?

Sometimes called near-rhyme, lazy rhyme, or slant rhyme, is a type of rhyme formed by words with similar but not identical sounds. In most instances, either the vowel segments are different while the consonants are identical, or vice versa. This type of rhyme is also called approximate rhyme, inexact rhyme, imperfect rhyme (in contrast to perfect rhyme), off rhyme, analyzed rhyme, suspended rhyme, or sprung rhyme.

See if you can **FIND** the words that are not so perfect like Tupelo.

Many, many years ago,
I met a gal,
and her name was Jo.
In the early stages of
getting to know,
she mentioned her small
apartment and a black cat
named **Tupelo**.

TUPELO · TUPELO · TUPELO · TUPELO

"Not just any black cat,"
she emphatically said,
"but a Norwegian Forest Cat,
with big yellow eyes
and wild black hair
from the tip of his tail
to the top of his head.
He is old and cranky,
and at times quite mean,
he growls and hisses,
and sometimes I scream.
At times he is friendly
but slow to warm,
too much attention,
and I'll get a scratch on my arm."

I began to think back
to when I was young,
we had dogs and cats,
and we all got along.
Dogs run and jump
and go all day;
wagging tails and wet kisses,
they just want to play.
But a cat's affection can
be quite a puzzle.
They give love when they want
with loud purrs and a nuzzle.
Cats are content and do
fine on their own,
independent and fussy;
it's very well known.

When I was older,
I had a roommate named Barnie,
we adopted a cat
and called him "Arnie."
For over a year
we lived with that feline,
and for quite a while,
life was just fine.
And then one day,
as most things prove,
a change came about,
and we had to move.
My roommate left
for another state,
and I had to give up the cat
– what would become of his fate?

I frantically searched to
find the cat a new home.
I couldn't let the poor guy
end up alone.
After several weeks and
time running thin,
I thought I had failed
and was about to give in.
But at the last minute,
a friend came to my aid;
she said, "I'll adopt Arnie,"
my worst fears allayed.
And when he was gone,
I felt sad in my heart,
but I was so glad he'd
found a fresh start.

Later in life, working hard
and buckling down,
I managed a restaurant on
the outskirts of town.
One summer day
by a patio tree,
a stray Calico appeared,
and the staff named her CC.
She was quite skittish
and very shy;
when we tried to pet her,
she would run off and hide.

In time she began
to warm to our touch,
and after a few months,
she let us pick her up.
When winter came,
we bought her
a small house of her own,
complete with a tiny heater
to warm the cozy home.
As time went by,
she became our communal pet;
we even took her for checkups
and shots at the vet.
Several years later,
the time had arisen,
a change of path, a new job,
and a new position.
From time to time,
I thought of that stray;
CC had adopted us
– not the other way.

Now back to my story
of when I met Jo
and the bushy black cat
named Tupelo.
The time had come to
meet the cat;
I was excited and nervous,
as a matter of fact.
With long wiry hair,
he looked pretty frumpy,
and it was matted in places,
no wonder he was grumpy.
"He's very skittish,"
she dutifully warned,
and sure enough
– a loud growl,
then a scratched arm.
A few more dates
with a similar ending,
growls, hisses, and scratches
– and I would need mending.

Spending more time
with me became
a pattern for Jo.
On most weekends,
her apartment sat empty
– except for the black cat
named Tupelo.
I had nothing against the cat,
it was just easier for us,
my house was more
comfortable,
without all the fuss.

As the years flew by,
there became a new need
– a house was purchased
for Jo and me.
But before moving,
we went back to and fro
about what we should
do with Tupelo.
He didn't really like me,
and he was also quite hairy;
shedding, scratches,
and blood
– it all began to scare me!
But Jo assured to my chagrin,
she'd get him shaved
at the groomer
to keep his hair trimmed.

And so, we all moved in
on a crisp fall day,
the cat, Jo, and I
would try to find a way.
Jo was a schoolteacher,
I worked from home,
and for most of the day,
it was just the cat and me
– all alone.
As I worked in my office
day to day,
Tupelo wandered in
– looked around
– and sometimes
– stay?

But when I tried to pet him,
he'd seem fine for an instant,
then hisses, growls,
and scratches
– followed by disinfectant.
As the fall season progressed,
his coat became quite thick,
then Jo took him to the groomer
– that sure did the trick!
After his shave,
he mostly was bare,
except for his tail and paws
and a mane of thick hair.

We whistled and laughed
with playful pokes;
Tupelo's new haircut
was the butt of our jokes.
As fall gave to winter,
and since he was very old,
we gave him a blanket
to fend off the cold.
As winter progressed,
his hair grew in;
I was getting scratched less
– which was definitely a win!

The winter months passed,
and one fine spring morning,
Jo looked at Tupelo and said,
"It's time for another shoring."
So off he went
to the groomer again,
to get the same haircut
 – and the jokes began to begin.
Only this time was different
when he came home,
he was undoubtedly mad
at what had been done.

We tried to pet him,
but he hissed,
and he growled;
his attitude towards us
most definitely fouled!
Jo cried and screamed,
"My cat hates my guts!"
I tried to console her,
but she thought I was nuts.
And sure enough,
time faded and blurred,
and he was back in her arms
where he heartily purred.

We decided against
another close shave,
then something strange happened,
he preened,
and he groomed,
and better yet
- started to behave?
He lingered in my office
more each day,
often for hours
– taking naps
– and even play.
As he warmed up,
so did I,
and a bond started to form
– one couldn't deny.

Then one day at the store,
I had a great thought,
Tupelo probably likes sardines,
so that's what I bought.
When I got home
and cracked open the tin,
his big yellow eyes grew
– and then he dove in!
At that point,
I had a new friend,
and I looked forward
to seeing him
again and again.

I stocked up on sardines,
tuna, and treats,
so my new pal had many
good things to eat.
Then one night,
while watching T.V.,
Tupelo jumped on the sofa
and laid down next to me.
I glanced at Jo
just before bed,
when all of a sudden
– he licked my forehead?

We giggled and laughed
at his display of affection;
from that time on,
there'd be a new direction.
Our bond grew and grew
as time went by,
this bushy black cat
constantly by my side.
Aside from the loud purr
and the bushy black hair,
this cat was quite different,
with attitude to spare.
He'd meow and meow
as if he could talk,
then lead me away
– out the front door
for a walk?

One night while sleeping
contently in bed,
I awoke to his paw
gently poking my head.
I looked at Jo,
and she was fast asleep,
so I rose from bed
with hardly a peep.
On came the hall lights
and the kitchen soon after;
I wondered where he was,
and more importantly
– what was the matter?

Then I found him
sitting alone in the tub,
looking up at me as if to say,
"Hey!
- *Turn on the faucet, bub!"*
So, I turned on the water
very low,
then Tupelo drank,
lapping the flow.
I chuckled and chortled
and snorted with glee;
I'd never seen
a cat drink water
to such a degree.

Eventually, the time came
when we needed a break,
after working non-stop,
a vacation we'd take.
It was only a few days
that we would be gone;
surely the cat
would be fine on his own?
While we were away,
my thoughts started to creep,
about Tupelo home alone
– why it was even hard to sleep.

I became very sad
as I thought way back
– to all those years
in the dark apartment
– alone in the black.
I couldn't wait to get home
to my bushy friend;
I would make up for lost time
– I'd make amends!

My days with the cat
were never dull,
taking walks and eating sardines
till our bellies were full.
As time drifted by,
Tupelo slowed and aged;
we knew it was getting close
to turn the page.
He was quite old,
and soon evident he might die,
in his final days,
we were distraught
and woefully cried.
With his last breath on earth,
we were laden with sorrow,
then the black cat passed,
there'd be no tomorrow.
I found solace thinking
of how he changed my life
and the fun days
without all the strife.

And I guess there's a moral,
I hope you can see,
pets need attention
to be all they can be.
If you own a pet,
nurture them and care,
through the good and bad times,
barking, scratches, and hair.
Just like humans,
they need kindness and love
– to be free and felt needed
– so they can rise above.
And that's the story
about me and Jo,
and how I became pals
with a big black cat
named **Tupelo**.

The author resides in Salt Lake City, Utah, with Jo and two tomcats - Tucker, a classic orange Tabby, and Max Skinner, an American shorthair.

Pictures of both cats were used in the book – can you find them?

www.ingramcontent.com/pod-product-compliance
Lightning Source LLC
Chambersburg PA
CBHW040320100526
44583CB00004BB/164